SYRIA

The United Nations on Vacation

By
Harvey Carroll, Jr.
"THE UNELECTED PRESIDENT"

Copyright © 2016 Harvey Carroll, Jr.

This is my book on Libya. I have written a near 30 page Poem on "Desert Storm." Books include a Mini-Autobiography "THE UNELECTED PRSIDENT), SCREWED, which is about the Lewinsky sex scandal and my involvement in Clinton's "Little White House Lie," and my "Operation Just Cause; "my suggestion for the Panama Invasion, my helping to organize and maintain the 1st Gulf War "Desert Storm" my missionary mission turned military mission; hence, "Black Hawk Down," Libya and my suggestions for U.N. "Humanitarian Intervention" and this book on Syria that was somewhat affected by the Libyan "Humanitarian Intervention" failures...

I intend to publish a series of Books under the trademark "THE UNELECTED PRESIDENT"

ISBN-13:
978-1530132935

ISBN-10:
1530132932

DEDICATION

This book is dedicated to those working with The United Nations and Global Citizens that work daily paid and unpaid to help develop constructive policy leadership, and it is also dedicated to the millions of displaced people from the countries discussed within this book.

.

ACKNOWLEDGMENTS

I wish to thank my friends and family for being patient with me... I know I spend a great deal of time focusing on the World and less on them... I am sorry for that, but I have noticed what happens to others often reflect how our own lives are better or worse... We should try to do better to get better...

INTRODUCTION

My Expert Opinion on Syria, Terrorism and United Nations Partner Policy Making...

In short I have followed the Syrian issue since the beginning. I feel that my United Nations "Humanitarian Intervention" into Libya had quite an impact on the "Failed Policies" that occurred in Syria after a Russian VETO in the United Nations Security Council. Russia grandstanded about how Gadhafi was brutally killed and how the U.N. overstepping authority of the resolution.

This compares and contrast Libya with Syria and we see that despite Libya turning into a failed state the "Humanitarian Intervention" did not follow my suggestions completely, nor did U.N. accept a "Divide Libya" Policy it still outweighs the support of al Assad's "Mass Murders" and a 5 year Civil War that has cost nearly 350,000 lives and about 4.5 million refugees fleeing Syria...

Negotiations continue "5 Years later" with Secretary of State Kerry leading the way...

1
SYRIA/al ASSAD
UN PARTNER TURNED PARASITE.

This book is about Syria and the problems that have led to more than 350,000 people being killed, and over 4.5 million refugees that have fled Syria; however, we cannot talk about Syria, without recognizing that "Humanitarian Intervention" into Libya had influence on what occurred in Syria.

I'll briefly sum up this, and focus more on these influences in the Chapter, pertaining to the US led, United Nations "Humanitarian Intervention" into Libya.

I'm also writing a more detailed book about my involvement in making suggestions to encourage the United Nations to provide "Humanitarian Intervention" into Libya.

For now let's just jump into this book, but realize that "Humanitarian Intervention" into Libya led to issues in Syria...

I'm writing this because I was somewhat involved long before trouble began in Syria... It actually began from my suggestions to encourage the "United Nations to provide "Humanitarian Intervention" in Libya.

I will then discuss how the Russian VETO in the United Nations Security Council in support of Assad/Syria came about. After that I will give you my opinion that Russia has supported Mass Murders in both Syria and Ukraine and how important it is for Russia to focus on humanity and be a partner in the United Nations.

This book will voice my great concerns for a "Grand Coalition Intervention in Syria to reduce Terrorism is not well thought out.

The coalition concept is being compared to my helping with planning, and organizing the multinational coalition during the 1st Gulf War; however, there was a lot of thought that went into the 1st Gulf War.

I do not see the same attention being put into Syrian Policy Making. In fact I favor the need for more brains than bombs and boots on the ground in Syria, and the need to reach out to the Muslim community to focus on the reality that radical Muslim's are becoming monsters as opposed to martyrs and are in essence contrary to God...

Often policy makers too act contrary to God and show little in the way of humanity. I on the other hand at least tried to ask what would God do or like to see happened...

Therefore, I favor a "Diplomatic Delegation to Syria and Jordan "in the initial stages of Syria's move towards Civil War…

Jordan, like usual, in my opinion is the most reasonable, and could have hosted Delegations to prevent War… Granted most every regional player wants change, but no one knows what it takes to make change happen… Nor are they focused on "Constructive Change."

Democracy is about presenting sound Political, Economic, and Social, Technological - Transportation, and Legal (PESTEL) reforms via Professional Public Administration Policy, as opposed to Destructive Leadership and/or Democracy.

"Might is right" and the strongman rules cannot, nor should not become the policy making mechanism…

I watched part of Syrian President Assad's General Assembly Address and in many ways I felt sorry for Assad, and the position he was in; however, I had great reservations on what he was leading his country into and it turned out to be far worse than the World expected...

Assad was very wishy-washy on several points. Disorganized and jumped from point to point. His back and forth--weak to strong nationalism rhetoric to rally his base supporters quickly isolated the rest of his country, especially after he began barrel bombing peaceful protesters in several cities...

All in all it was perplexing, and disturbing to see him try to make his "Dictatorial Leadership" case fully blaming problems he created on external influence.

Granted I can also see that those allegations have some merit, as Syria is a "Proxy Country" that could easily develop or destroy itself without crafty leadership... But, unlike Jordanian leadership, al-Assad ruled with ruthless unreasonable approaches as opposed to reason and respect for the people of his nation...

It was up to Secretary of State Clinton's Diplomacy to try and solve those issues, via "Reset Policies "and other Diplomatic tools; however, old "Cold War" crazy got in the way.

Proxy Syria was plunged into Civil Conflict after Assad became a "Mass Murder," fully supported by Russia's Putin and Medvedev, whom also supported the brutal Mass Murders of the Yanukovych regime in Ukraine...

President Assad pushing an external threat trying to make himself and Syria the "Victim of a Global Conspiracy" was fueled from a decade of failed Bush Policies, SOFA Agreements and the like that had helped to destabilize the Middle East, and Global Economy…

While President Assad's statements gained some merit in the region, fueled by the Blundering Bush policies that pointed towards Syria when they could find any WMD's in Iraq.

Most Americans as well as the World realize Bush was wrong in his reasoning for returning to Iraq; however, the Defense hawks, placed Syria in their cross-hairs.

Assad had a couple roads he could have taken. The high road could have united his country, while the low road took him down with Gadhafi, and others that were in conflict with America/West as opposed to focusing on internal reforms...

Assad left America with little room to take the high road either. So, America had to play its part also. Granted we could have recognized that we have victimized Syria via mistakes, and bad intelligence in our bravado attack on a Saddam Hussein, even if Saddam was a "Pain in the Arse" for nearly two decades, the return to Iraq was not justified, nor were the accounts of WMD's in Iraq.

Even the Assad regime recognized that Saddam had taken every opportunity to push the West too far. On several occasions Saddam Hussein tried to involve Syria, and/or provoke Israel and the Palestinians in attempts to broaden Iraq's power base.

Syrian leadership did not fall for it. Syria ignored attempts by Saddam Hussein, and they dealt well with Israel, and Israel respected their Air Space, which brought Syria into the multinational coalition during the 1st Gulf War.

Both Syria and Jordan have been partners and deserve more respect and appreciation by the West... I for one respected what they had done to maintain peace, especially Jordan's former King Hussein...

I strongly supported "Reforms over Revolutions," yet, I and most of the World had to support "Peaceful Protest" of Democracy voices over Dictatorial slave states in Syria, Ukraine, Egypt, Tunisia and others...

With that said, Revolutionaries could have been turned into Professional Public Administrators via PESTEL policies, as opposed to Pistil policies... With a bit of acceptable PESTEL "Reforms" from Assad AND assistance such as my suggestion for a UN "Global Reform Mandate"

I supported a strong Jordanian led Delegation at the beginning of the Syrian civil war and continue to support such a delegation still today...

Assad's speech, with the basic high lights:

2
ME, THE U.S.A, AND THE UNITED NATIONS "REPUTATION AND CREDIBILITY"

Reputation and Credibility as a person, a nation or acting collectively as The United Nations has to establish "Reputation and Credibility" to be affective...

I would like to take the first chapter of the book to instill the important value of a sound Reputation and Credibility as a Policy Maker; and how that affects me as a Global Citizens, America and/or the United Nations.

I will then compare and contrast that with the lack of a sound Reputation and Credibility and show how not working more closely with the United Nations minimized the International Communities ability to solve problems in Syria...

The Value of a sound Reputation and Credibility as a Policy Maker:

First my "Reputation and Credibility;" I have a good solid Education holding a Bachelors of Business Administration specializing in Real Estate and Finance (helped Develop 10's of Millions of Dollars' worth of Real Estate Projects), Masters work in Business, Public Administration, as well as Diplomacy and International Commerce.

My Political Junkie experiences have many success stories at the local, state, national and international levels; thereby, developing vast improvements at all levels and even resulted in the saving of millions of lives and positively affecting the economic fate of nations.

Obviously, people question this as they ask where the money, where is your list of offices held, and/or government positions/jobs...

Applying honestly is as unbelievable as the statements itself... Land Development is high profile, and the margins of money to be made are not that great, and the business is often boom and bust, especially in the more recent economic downturns... Then try to balance business with the calling for political policy making and it isn't that profitable, but I survived...

In politics is not all about being elected by special interest, it is about being affective in the important issues. Be it simple City Revitalization, influencing new roads, bridges, by-pass, community centers, or industrial parks.

On the State level influencing funding for Education Equalization (KERA), and then the National Level helping solve economic issues and/or providing insight for International issues to include wars and strategy that will save lives and positively affect global economies. All of which are not that tough if you find the right people to reach out to and communicate effectively with, just as this letter is reaching you today...

I used to get very tired of people challenging my "reputation and credibility", then I begin to welcome a discussions about my "reputation and credibility" and my key character traits that increased the effectiveness of carrying out leadership, economic statecraft and/or any political policy; be it at the local, state, national or international level.

I think this debate can bring value to me, America and the World...

Reputation and Credibility are two concepts that are interrelated when it comes to influencing policy. In a humble way I would like to say that I have always had a strong mind despite dealing with decades of PTSD, and had great faith that I could do what I set out to do.

Such thinking and belief has allowed me to constructively shape policy that I felt should be changed... At the end of the day, it came down to me having the faith and will to follow through. I as a policy-maker have grown to not having to justify everything in my past. I now feel that I have gained a solid Reputation and Credibility and I work hard to back up what I say.

Fellow Policy Makers can quickly look at my background and make the determination if I have a solid Reputation and Credibility or not and determine if they fell I can add value to the Policy Making process.

Reputation and Credibility of my past performance is pretty well documented to the point to determine that I as a policy-maker; "the sender" to be a real tiger and not a paper tiger...

Similarly, credibility should provoke a sense of no doubt in the targets mind that as a policy-maker that I would certainly be able to follow through with any stated threat, and/or any economic development plan that I would endorse.

On the other hand if I feel the Policy is bad I say so as I did with the return to Iraq by George W. Bush. I clearly stated that I believed the U.N. Weapons Inspectors that there were no WMD's in Iraq and no justification for war.

President Obama also clearly voiced his lack of support for that conflict. Yet, he did not have the insight that I had as I had helped organize and maintain the multi-national coalition during the 1st Gulf War; thereby, saving millions of lives and affecting the economic fate of nations.

These for strategies that brought about a quick end to the war (4 days, and 4 hours) as opposed to dilly dallying around in the desert for decades squandering trillions, and prevented it from spreading and destabilizing the region as we see after the return to Iraq by George W. Bush...

The lack of a solid Reputation and Credibility as a person and America:

As I mentioned in the past I struggled with the lack of a solid Reputation and Credibility as a Policy-maker; however, that is nothing in compared to the damage that George W. Bush did to America's Reputation and Credibility.

America armed with the strongest military on earth, the strongest economic statecraft tools. Even without the World Trade Center post 9/11 the U.S. remained the number one economy with the most credible business rule of law in the World, but declined in many ways, even with myself and others trying to prevent the more rapid decline.

This economic statecraft power has allowed the United States Policy Makers to collect thoughts of people like myself to impose sanctions with the support of the International Community in Iran, Russia and other hotspots around the World.

However, Sanctions rarely work as it only makes stronger ties with other nations that counter U.S. policy as we see now in Iran as well as their support in Syria as our policy-making ability to compel the Syrian and Iranian Governments to do what we wanted them to do is was undermined by Russia whom we provided AID to post Soviet Collapse.

China which depends on America and Western European friends to maintain its economy represents about ½ of America's Trillion dollar trade imbalance... So, we also provided a stable economy for China... China's State Run Economy has placed America in some difficult trade policy dilemmas. We must really take a look at these trade policies in the future...

The Bush blunders, along with Senator McConnell's continued push to raise debt ceilings; thereby, borrowing from his Wife's home country of China has undermined America's economic and national security as well as vastly undermining America's Reputation and Credibility, and its ability to strongly use "Economic Statecraft Tools"...

I feel that I as a policy-maker I should strive to lead by example have integrity and always "say what I mean, and mean what I say". In doing so, for nearly three decades developed a tract record of accomplishing amazing policies both foreign and domestic. Yet, I have seen Washington Policy Makers undermine such virtues that America once held dearly. The simple "Freedom, Truth and Justice"... All deteriorated American leadership...

I feel that I have established a strong reputation and credibility with my constituents throughout world and feel God would approve of my values to preserve the sanctity of humanity. I have come to peace with my inner-self as my policies in the past have cost lives in the pursuit of trying to keep conflicts from getting out of control.

I feel that I have developed a sound Reputation and credibility and used them as strong leverage tools in effecting sound policy, and shaping a constructive and more peaceful and prosperous world.

As a policy-maker I challenge you to join me to also have a profound effect on Diplomacy, Development and the promotion of Human Rights for a more peaceful and prosperous world. I also encourage you to realize the difficulties that Diplomats/Policy Makers have to deal with in their personal Reputation and Credibility.

American policy makers have to bring value and honest appreciation for America's Reputation and Credibility... Yet, we cannot get there if we do not recognize that our nation's Reputation and Credibility has declined, but we can regain it by taking the moral high ground and clearly pointing out the humanitarian aspects of policy making starting with Syria..

Now, you decide if my reputation and credibility as a policy-maker has gained your support and trust. If so then join me in articulating the need to try to bring Political and Economic Stability to America, as well as the Middle East/Africa, Russia and Ukraine and other hot spots in the World by being a voice of reason...

3
MY SUGGESTIONS
FOR
UNITED NATIONS
"HUMANITARIAN INTERVENTION"
INTO LIBYA

As Global Citizens we should strive to solve problems, as opposed to becoming part of the problem...

In my attempt to solve problems in Libya, resulted in becoming part of the problem in Syria...

Citizens and Diplomats alike should realize that the key is to focus on long-term constructive policy development and not go for the short-term political soundbites for TV...

We simply have to make it clear that problems in the World or the problems in our lives rarely get solved quickly.

We must focus our time and attention; therefore, we must realize that the same time and attention has to be focused on solving very big problems around the world and the need for the best and brightest to dedicate years of their lives to solve such problems...

Solving the problem requires Diplomats, Department of Commerce-- Professional Public Administrator armed with "Comprehensive Planning Templates" that encourage Civil Society/Global Citizens to participate in creating growth and development, while adding more quality of life.

This type of focus makes great improvements to Local, Regional, State, and International Business must look at Public Private Partnership's opportunities to maintain political and economic stability...

Diplomats, the Department of Commerce and Professional Administrators armed with "Comprehensive Planning Templates" must work together to create long term planning.

Local, Regional, State, as well as National and International Business must look at ways to expand Public Private Partnership opportunities. Business is the driver of the real economy that maintains political and economic stability...

The Results will be far more affective in the long run...

Now I will give you an example of how both Libyan and Syrian policy making came about and why such care and attention must be used to develop constructive policy making...

--Sadly, my constructive suggestions for "Humanitarian Intervention" into Libya went a bit extreme; as opposed to my "Divide Libya Policy" the U.S. Ambassador Stevens armed Benghazi and other Rebels (it got himself killed as

I warned could happen via fb to his fellow Diplomat--Sr. Clinton/Obama Advisor).

U.S. President Obama and Secretary of State Clinton gave into the Hawks of Washington and began calling for Gadhafi regime change ultimately led to the Ambassador and fellow Diplomats death... Yet, this was not totally their fault as the Republicans would like to make people believe.

Granted Gadhafi returned to his old way of being a bad Dictator, whom was leading his military on a murderous massacre into Misrata, and headed towards Benghazi in the East, but there was a Diplomatic window of opportunity that may have been able to prevent this if regime change had not become the norm...

I truly believe a more constructive "Divide Libya" policy could have prevented Civil Conflict in Libya... Yet, rhetoric in America during the Political Presidential race set reason aside that focused on short term as opposed to long term constructive Policy Making...

This United Nations overkill, which not only destroyed Gadhafi's Army-also led to the brutal and inhumane killing of Gadhafi. This brutal international display of inhumane death of the dictator touched even the strongest hawk hearts and minds.

The Gadhafi killing allowing Putin and Medvedev of Russia to cite Libya as a failure, as did Republican hawks, which President Obama had caved into in favor of regime change... I had great concerns for "Regime Change" in Libya and strongly voiced this to international political think tanks such as "The Council on Foreign Relations (CFR)."

I noticed that Dr. Haass of the CFR echoed my concerns to the Senate Hearing chaired by then Senator Kerry.

The talk of hasty "Regime Change" in Libya led to series of unreasonable outcomes; Syria is one of them...

I think that U.S. Secretary of State Clinton was somewhat between the Hawks and constructive policy makers. Yet, I think she was well aware that Gadhafi had a brutal history; thereby, giving our U.S. Ambassador to Libya a lot of leeway, which allowed him to work more closely with the Department of Defense military minds to Arm rebel's...

This leeway that Secretary of State Clinton placed the Ambassador Steven's fate into the hands of the Defense hawks that failed to protect him...

4
RE: PUTINS LETTER TO THE NEW YORK TIMES...
A REMINDER TO RUSSIAN PRESIDENT PUTIN THAT RUSSIA RECEIVED "AMERICAN HUMANITARIAN INTERVENTION" TO STABALIZE RUSSIA POST SOVIET COLLAPSE.

"The following chapter is is copied verbatim from the New York Times; I then added my thoughts as if I were replying to Putin......."
Oliver Munday

A Plea for Caution From Russia
What Putin Has to Say to Americans About Syria

By VLADIMIR V. PUTIN
Published: September 11, 2013

MOSCOW -Putin— RECENT events surrounding Syria have prompted me to speak directly to the American people and their political leaders. It is important to do so at a time of

27

insufficient communication between our societies.

Putin-Relations between us have passed through different stages. We stood against each other during the cold war. But we were also allies once, and defeated the Nazis together. The universal international organization — the United Nations — was then established to prevent such devastation from ever happening again.

Harvey-This is true, however, at that time I had spent weeks written a number of papers that tried to remind Russia that a U.S. led "Humanitarian Intervention" vastly helped Russia and other former Soviet States post collapse...

Putin-The United Nations' founders understood that decisions affecting war and peace should happen only by consensus, and with America's consent the veto by Security Council permanent members was enshrined in the United Nations Charter. The profound wisdom of this has underpinned the stability of international relations for decades.

Harvey-I would not completely agree with this statement; America has provided great leadership in the past and we have also made mistakes... However, Russia has not shown wisdom in Syria. While the United States and the U.N. may have made a few mistakes with "Humanitarian Intervention" in Libya the "Do Nothing" policy of Russian Veto's in the Security Council has led to over 350,000 deaths, over 4.5 million war refugees on the welfare of the United Nations. All of which are living in horrible conditions...

Putin-No one wants the United Nations to suffer the fate of the League of Nations, which collapsed because it lacked real leverage. This is possible if influential countries bypass the United

Nations and take military action without Security Council authorization.

Harvey-It would be very bad to lose the United Nations. Yet, we have to look at this statement in two ways. Putin favors the United Nations, but failed to work with the United Nations to take Constructive course of action during the Syrian Civil War to prevent vast bloodshed and millions fleeing Syria. The lack of action is also "Military Action"... In fact, Russia has supplied the Assad Regime with Weapons before and since the VETO; thereby, undermining the legitimacy of the United Nations... Russian guns are the weapons of choice for the Terrorist in the region as well. Most all of them are armed with Russian/old Soviet Block weapons...

Putin-The potential strike by the United States against Syria, despite strong opposition from many countries and major political and religious leaders, including the pope, will result in more innocent victims and escalation, potentially spreading the conflict far beyond Syria's borders. A strike would increase violence and unleash a new wave of terrorism. It could undermine multilateral efforts to resolve the Iranian nuclear problem and the Israeli-Palestinian conflict and further destabilize the Middle East and North Africa. It could throw the entire system of international law and order out of balance.

Harvey-"Humanitarian Intervention" in Libya ended such issues quickly... Russia's strong support and VETO in the United Nations has done exactly what he is writing about... I wrote about such issues nearly two years before the Putin letter... While I had initially hoped that Russia could have a "Constructive Influence" on the Syrian Regime it did the contrary and created the problems we see today... And the lack of constructive United Nations involvement will only it continue to get worse in Syria...

Putin-Syria is not witnessing a battle for democracy, but an armed conflict between government and opposition in a multi-religious country. There are few champions of democracy in Syria. But there are more than enough Qaeda fighters and extremists of all stripes battling the government. The United States State Department has designated Al Nusra Front and the Islamic State of Iraq and the Levant, fighting with the opposition, as terrorist organizations. This internal conflict, fueled by foreign weapons supplied to the opposition, is one of the bloodiest in the world.

Harvey-I have to call "Bull Sh!t" on this statement... When the United States first asked for the United Nations to take a serious look at Syria it was a Democracy Movement... In fact, I wrote a number of letters suggesting "Diplomatic Delegations" to go to Syria to discuss a

Constructive Diplomatic Solution to prevent Civil War... Instead, the Russians held firm support for the Assad regime and Assad begin indiscriminate bombings of various religious regions that brought a lot of hatred from all over Syria into the fight... While Assad blamed outside influence he was bombing Cities within Syria adding fuel to the flames...

Putin-Mercenaries from Arab countries fighting there, and hundreds of militants from Western countries and even Russia, are an issue of our deep concern. Might they not return to our countries with experience acquired in Syria? After all, after fighting in Libya, extremists moved on to Mali. This threatens us all.

Harvey-War anywhere threatens Humanity... As mentioned above Libya was a great "Humanitarian Intervention" case as compared to the clustered mess of following the Russian

VETO within the Security Council over the past two years... It was only after years of fighting and attacks in Paris that a rise of Terrorism occurred in Mali. One has to wonder if Russia was not supporting such uprisings in Mali since he was writing about them years before...

Putin-From the outset, Russia has advocated peaceful dialogue enabling Syrians to develop a compromise plan for their own future. We are not protecting the Syrian government, but international law. We need to use the United Nations Security Council and believe that preserving law and order in today's complex and turbulent world is one of the few ways to keep international relations from sliding into chaos. The law is still the law, and we must follow it whether we like it or not. Under current international law, force is permitted only in self-defense or by the decision of the Security Council. Anything else is unacceptable under the

United Nations Charter and would constitute an act of aggression.

Harvey-Russia has failed to act on the best interest of the International Community and that of the Syrians by turning a blind eye to the Assad Regime's "Mass Murders"... Russia's VETO gave the Assad Regime a Green Light to a path of over 350,000 deaths and over 4.5 Million War Refugees that are cold, hungry and now being cared for and fed by the International Community that cannot keep up with the needs of so many refugees... It wouldn't surprise me if they failed to fund the feeding of the 2 million children in the Refugee Camps... I don't see Putin eager to give Political Asylum to the 4.5 million Refugees caused by the lack of Russian Leadership at the United Nations... Putin thought writing this was providing Leadership to the World... The word "Delusional" comes to my mind... We see the results of Putin policy making...

Putin-No one doubts that poison gas was used in Syria. But there is every reason to believe it was used not by the Syrian Army, but by opposition forces, to provoke intervention by their powerful foreign patrons, who would be siding with the fundamentalists. Reports that militants are preparing another attack — this time against Israel — cannot be ignored.

Harvey- Syrian position was they there was no Chemical Weapons within Syria. This Flip-Flop of Policy is called a "LIE"... It is also ironic that Putin called Secretary Kerry a liar, when in fact Putin has clearly been caught in a Lie... This undermines his Reputation and Credibility and pretty much makes the letter to the New York Times as worthless in my opinion... Strait out from the old KGB Book of BS...

Putin-It is alarming that military intervention in internal conflicts in foreign countries has become commonplace for the United States. Is it in America's long-term interest? I doubt it. Millions around the world increasingly see America not as a model of democracy but as relying solely on brute force, cobbling coalitions together under the slogan "you're either with us or against us."

Harvey-This is a 1/2 truth... I too, as well as President Obama opposed the Bush led coalition into Iraq. The false dichotomy of "you're either with us or against us" has the world at hesitation; however, the lack of Today's Leadership failing to lead in a constructive way is the question that we should be pondering in the United Nations and not failed leadership of the past that Americans and the world are clearly aware of... I voiced my opposition to a return to Iraq during the George W. Bush Administration. Yet, I understood that Saddam continued to defy the International Community; thereby, giving the extra push that resulted in his demise... A demise that cost America Trillions of Dollars since 2000 as well as diminishing trust... I reflect back during the 1st Gulf War when I helped organize and maintain the multi-national coalition... I might add that I also put words in President Gorbachev's mouth via a Classified deal that tried to prevent war; however, it did not influence Saddam to back out of Kuwait; unfortunately, the support to guarantee Iraq's borders failed and that led to a war that diminished Saddam's Army that would have eventually cost millions of lives and vastly diminished the economic fate of nations... These Intelligence Reviews were always in the minds of Intelligence Agents and as the Middle East become more problematic saw that Saddam could again return to center stage...

Putin-But force has proved ineffective and pointless. Afghanistan is reeling, and no one can say what will happen after international forces withdraw.

Libya is divided into tribes and clans. In Iraq the civil war continues, with dozens killed each day. In the United States, many draw an analogy between Iraq and Syria, and ask why their government would want to repeat recent mistakes.

Harvey-Long Term Conflict is Costly and can be very ineffective and pointless; this point I have to agree... My coalition during the 1st Gulf War resulted in a conflict that lasted 100 hours (4 days, and 4 hours); thereby, saving millions of lives and positively affecting the economic fate of nations... The blundering Bush return did lead to long term occupation issues in both Iraq and Afghanistan and I have written a number of position papers expressing this...   After the "Red Line" use of "Chemical Weapons" that killed nearly 1,500 Syrians; 500 of which were sleeping children."   I suggested that President Obama use military force in Syria, much like I suggested during the

1st Gulf War... I also suggest President Obama do this via the United Nations and the International Criminal Court and indict Assad on 5 Counts... I will address these in this book a bit more...

Putin-No matter how targeted the strikes or how sophisticated the weapons, civilian casualties are inevitable, including the elderly and children, whom the strikes are meant to protect.

Harvey-The question the Security Council has to ask its self "Does the End Justify the Means"... The "Humanitarian Intervention" in Libya ended a Civil War quickly; it also led to the death of Gadhafi... I supported a "Divide Libya" plan along with my suggestion for "Humanitarian Intervention"; however, if we take a clear look at the "Humanitarian Intervention" in Libya we have to recognize that it resulted in only a hand full of War Refugees as compared to the 2 million that have fled

Syria today as well as the near 5 million displaced within the country. Then the amount of deaths is a fraction of the 350,000 reported within Syria to date and the 4.5 million refugees that are cold and hungry, many on foot for hundreds of miles to Europe... The body count and war refugees will be greater without real Security Council "Humanitarian Intervention"...

Putin-The world reacts by asking: if you cannot count on international law, then you must find other ways to ensure your security. Thus a growing number of countries seek to acquire weapons of mass destruction. This is logical: if you have the bomb, no one will touch you. We are left with talk of the need to strengthen nonproliferation, when in reality this is being eroded.

Harvey-This is exactly the United States concern... This is why the United States has asked Russia to be a responsible member of the United Nations Security

Council. Instead they have slacked on North Korea and Iran's quest for Nuclear Weapons. In fact, Russian contractors are participating in building the facility in Iran. This Russian Oligarch system of Government Mafiaism might work in Russia but it threatens progress in Russia, Peace in the World and degrades Humanity...

In the past I have taken a lot of flak from suggesting that the United States come to the AID of Russia post-Soviet Collapse. I suggested supplying AID in exchange for dismantling Nuclear Weapons to prevent the 15 former Soviet States from falling into a state of war, using Nuclear Weapons against each other. My thoughts were to also to secure such arsenals to prevent them from ending up on the black market and into terrorist hands... Now, after nearly three decades of constructive U.S./Russia relations that reduced the threat of Nuclear Weapons, Russia VETO's and/or fails to act responsibly within the United Nations Security Council to place such weapons under the control of the United Nations and/or provide United Nations Control of safe nuclear power...

Putin-We must stop using the language of force and return to the path of civilized diplomatic and political settlement.

Harvey-When will a voice of reason be looked at as opposed to Oligarch's interest in weapon sales. When will Russia that supports Oligarchy over Citizens Interest begin to serve their own interest over fellow Citizens interest and the Citizens of the World's best interest to progress Humanity?

Putin-A new opportunity to avoid military action has emerged in the past few days. The United States, Russia and all members of the international community must take advantage of the Syrian government's willingness to place its chemical arsenal under international control for subsequent destruction. Judging by the statements of President Obama, the United States sees this as an alternative to military action.

Harvey-I have to ask if this is a "Stall Tactic" strait from the old KGB book of BS? For I have dealt with the development of Biological and Chemical Weapons Burn Facilities. It takes months to inventory (longer in a war zone), then it takes years to build a facility in a responsible way and at a responsible site. (I recently posted a link on the U.S. Mission to the United Nations discussing the issues of building such a Burn Facility)... While this is a great concept of good will, unless there is an Immediate Stop to the Civil War it is unreasonable and will only turn out to be silliness... So, either Russia intends to stop the Civil War that they favored and in many ways founded by not acting responsibly in the

United Nations Security Council or it is all BS and just a Lie from Putin... We saw what was an area controlled by constructive opposition in the north of Syria basically divided by the highway from Baghdad to the Syrian coast in oppositions hands... Now that area is fractured and in ISIL/ISIS hands with a few factions of Turkmen that recently participated in shooting a Russian Pilot after a Russian fighter jet was shot down by Turkey after many Russian airspace violations...

Putin-I welcome the president's interest in continuing the duologue with Russia on Syria. We must work together to keep this hope alive, as we agreed to at the Group of 8 meeting in Lough Erne in Northern Ireland in June, and steer the discussion back toward negotiations.

Harvey-Talk is cheap, the U.S. and the World is looking for Action to stop the War Crimes being committed in Syria...

Putin-If we can avoid force against Syria, this will improve the atmosphere in international affairs and strengthen mutual trust. It will be our shared success and open the door to cooperation on other critical issues.

Harvey-There should be mutual trust as it was the United States led "Humanitarian Intervention" that came to the AID of Russia post-Soviet Collapse... So, I am not buying this argument... Accept the reality that the United States cares about constructive leadership and outcomes in the world.

Putin-My working and personal relationship with President Obama is marked by growing trust. I appreciate this. I carefully studied his address to the nation on Tuesday. And I would rather disagree with a case he made on American exceptionalism, stating that the United States' policy is "what makes America different. It's what makes us exceptional." It is extremely dangerous to encourage people to see themselves as exceptional, whatever the motivation. There are big countries and small countries, rich and poor, those with long democratic traditions and those still finding their way to democracy. Their policies differ, too. We are all different, but when we ask for the Lord's blessings, we must not forget that God created us equal.

Harvey-Again, after decades in the Cold War, it was the United States led "Humanitarian Intervention" via loans, buy-in of the Mir Space Station to convert it to the ISS International Space Station to continue technological advances, the reduction of nuclear threats; the dollar became the stabilizing currency in the bazaars/market place in Russia and other former Soviet States. American USAID, thousands of NGO's, Faith Based Organizations traveled to Russia to help and many are still there today... While Russians tried to keep those with great Business Skills out of the country in favor of oligarch's that bribe bankers, officials and the like to sell bad plans that are not based on sound economic and finance principles... All while Americans and other Westerners try to do honest business, follow and improve the Rule of Law and Civil Society in Russia/former Soviet States within Eastern Europe... I know I have spent over a decade traveling to the region and it is as crazy today as it was 11 years ago... Putin's voice of God is Krill that speaks for the Orthodox Church while wearing a $30,000 dollar Gold Rolex and together he and Putin jail's Pussy Riot for questioning Krill's statements of Putin being ordained by God; are they not equal to question such statements of the manipulation of faith?...

Vladimir V. Putin is the president of Russia.

I think this makes a lot of us American somewhat "exceptional" in our quest to serve and advance Humanity... This has been my slightly updated thoughts on Putin's letter.

I would like to end this chapter with several pages of thoughts reminding Putin that Russia was a huge recipient of American led "Humanitarian Intervention" into Russia and the former Soviet States, and to point out that it was the West that stabilized Russia, not him... The West, some of which were my ideas also prevented conflict within the former 15 Soviet States...

We tried it Russia's way in Syria for several years it hasn't worked; Russia sending troops and air support to shore up Assad only adds more hardships for the Syrian people...

I think it is important that the West remind Russia that they were recipients of American led International "Humanitarian Intervention" by myself, along with American USAID, hundreds of NGO's, thousands of Church/Faith Based Organizations, the Peace Corp and others came to the AID of Russia and the collapsed Soviet States... This "Humanitarian Intervention" Prevented War, keep Nuclear Weapons off the Black Market; thereby, saving Millions of Lives, and positively affecting the economic fate of nations...

Humanitarian Intervention post-Soviet Collapse prevented war amongst, and from within Russia and/or between the 15 Soviet States... After the collapse and breakup a number of my college professors and media accounts discussed the possibility of war within and amongst Soviet States over the quest for resources.

We can only imagine that money has become the equivalent of toilet paper, with less usefulness, no products on the store shelves and very high tensions at home and in the streets. This time of stress can easily lead to internal and external war. However, I and others made suggestions to supply AID to help our "Cold War" rivals that lasted over a 1/2 Century. This became reality as American Dollars become the stabilizing currency that facilitated translations and provided security and peace of mind for the masses.

This simple act of kindness of providing the "American Dollar" with the words "In God We Trust" as alternative currency prevented war and saved millions of lives. This policy has continued into recent years via IMF Loans and other Bank Bailouts that have keep people from going to the streets in violent armed protest... Yet, Russia is quick to forget about how American led "Humanitarian Intervention" helped stabilize and prevent conflict within and around Russia...

Humanitarian Intervention to keep Nuclear Weapons off the Black Market...

I had also suggested buying out the "Nuclear Stockpiles" to keep them off the Black Market. I could imagine a desperate Soviet Scientist or High Ranking Official selling a Nuclear Weapon to anyone willing to pay the price. We know from the film "Lord of War" that vast amounts of Soviet Weapons ended up all over the world and in some of the most ruthless people the world has seen. Nuclear Weapons would have also easily fallen into the hands of ruthless people.

Terrorist such as those that attacked American on 9/11 could have done a million times more damage to the economic and national security of the United States... While this was forethought, I also realized that weapons could have been put on the Black Market and used within Russia and/or other Soviet States; thereby, sparking nuclear confrontation within the former Soviet States and/or even worse they could have blamed the

United States, which could have led to Nuclear War.

Humanitarian Intervention in Russia and the other former Soviet States in Eastern Europe saved millions of lives, and positively affected the economic fate of nations... By preventing war and stabilizing the Russian/Eastern European Economies vast lives and economies were saved.

Not only were lives and economies saved but high tech industries, the space program such as my suggestion to buy into the Mir Space Station and convert it into the "International Space Station", which allowed the World to continue to benefit from Space and Technological Advances...

As a Humanitarian I recognized that people were probably much like me in America and just wanted to have a nice life. They wanted more than the basics of food, clothing and shelter. They too wished to get a good education, have a family, success and be able to pass that on to future generations. Yet, without a voice of reason and people like me suggesting to help Russia/Eastern Europe post collapse none of this would have been possible.

Russia should realize that they have been the recipient of American led "Humanitarian Intervention" that Prevented War, keep Nuclear Weapons off the Black Market; thereby, saving Millions of Lives, and affecting the economic fate of nations...

Russia and the former Soviet States without the American led "Humanitarian Intervention" would have been millions of times worse than the situation in Syria today., which has led to over 300 thousand killed by the al-Assad Regime, over 9 Million Displaced Syrians, 4.5 million of which have fled Syria and living in Refugee Camps (2 Million Children), the use of

Chemical Weapons that affected over 3 thousand people, 1,500 dead, which nearly 500 were children...

I hope that Russia will realize that the U.S. and the United Nations may have made a few mistakes in my suggestions to supply "Humanitarian Intervention" in Libya, but Russia's suggestions to stay out of Syria has led to hundreds of times more problems than a non "Humanitarian Intervention" policy.

Additional Resources:
http://blogs.voanews.com/russia-watch/2012/09/25/making-the-kremlin-queasy-massive-american-aid-has-helped-russians-three-times-in-the-last-century/

5
RUSSIAN VETO
IN THE
UNITED NATIONS SECURITY
COUNCIL IN SUPPORT OF ASSAD n
SYRIA, AND YANUKOVYCH MASS
MURDERS

The United Nations are not focusing on constructive policy making. It is becoming more of a "Grandstanding" podium than a place to solve problems...

The United Nations must work, or the world will see far worse problems than that occurring in Syria...

We see this with Russia's Putin and Medvedev's sided with Assad of Syria, as they did with the Yanukovych regime in Ukraine. Both positions are quite crazy as both the Syrian and Ukrainian regimes slaughtered "Peacefully Protesters" to try to maintain personal power...

In both Syria and Ukraine, I and a vast majority of the world favored "Peaceful Protest," and the hope of peaceful outcomes...

I as a Global Citizen wrote many position papers calling for power-sharing and/or the call for snap elections to prevent violence.

I also wrote and personally asked the U.S. Defense Attaché to work close with the Ukrainian Minister of Defense to ensure that the Army was not sent into the streets of Kiev. I knew if the Army was sent in that Yanukovych like al Assad would have no problem slaughtering peaceful protesters.

In Kiev, it could have resulted in 10's of thousands of Peaceful Protesters being killed... Fortunately, only Yanukovych Snipers were sent in that cost the lives of about 100 "The Heavenly Hundred"... The Ukrainian Minister of Defense had listened to the

American Defense Attaché', refused orders to send in the Army...

I strongly feel this decision saved 10's of thousands if not hundreds of thousands of people. For sure the Revolution would have started in Kiev a City of 4.5 million that would have torn apart...

I will not spend a great deal of time on Ukraine; however, I will mention that I am writing a book on Ukraine. The following photo is the draft cover. I will mention that both Ukraine and Syria's Heads of State failed to look at constructive leadership options. Both chose Mass Murder as their way of trying to hold onto power instead of simply working to serving the people. Granted Yanukovych was elected to serve, while al Assad was a Dictator that was self-serving, but both were quite similar... Both were self-serving.

"THE UNELECTED PRESIDENT"

UKRAINE

"Return to Revolution"

By
Harvey Carroll,
Jr.

At the end of the Ukrainian Revolution the Ukraine's President Yanukovych sent in Water Cannons and Snipers that killed the "Heavenly Hundred" and Syria slaughtered protesters and began bombing cities...

Both countries have ended up in conflict as a result of such brutal treatment of civilians, with Syria far more devastating at this time. Yet, if Russia continues on a destructive policy making path, it could lead to mass death and destruction in Ukraine... I know the mindset ant it is primed for such destruction, with few focusing on decentralization and reforms, or real plans to do either...

Fortunately, spending a great deal in Ukraine, I have managed to write position papers to continue the Democratic and peace promotion process. (Note, I was shocked that a Revolution occurred, and there was little Parliamentary actions that could have been taken to prevent mass corruption, and/or constructive trade negotiations.

Once the protest began those that I knew that were involved had a very difficult time. They were beaten, killed and in constant fear... I talked with some of them, and they wanted to arm themselves. While I understood their situation, I encouraged them to remain peaceful... I tried to remind them of great men like Gandhi, and Martin Luther King that led constructive peaceful "non-violent" protest and gained World support...

I also reminded them that they would all most likely be killed if they tried to arm themselves. The corrupt Yanukovych Administration was looking for any excuse to send in troops. If arms were found in the streets, he would certainly use it as an excuse to send in the Army...

I wrote and even called them many times encouraging them to stay peaceful, despite their continued complaints that they were being attacked and often beaten).

After the Revolution I tried to prevent Civil Conflict and advised caution on any Anti-Terror Operations to deal with the Russian backed Separatist in the East of Ukraine. The Separatist in the East began taking City and other Government Buildings by Armed Force...

I strongly believed that sharing the same thoughts that brought about the Revolution could be the solution to gain support of the people in Donetsk and Luhansk. Yet, this opportunity failed as Russia began to back the Separatists.

The new Ukrainian Government was failing in their offering of Decentralization of Political and Economic Reforms... The buzz word of "Reform, Reform, Reform, and Decentralization, Decentralization, Decentralization" became the talk of the region, but few knew how to do it...

I knew very well that it would take "Comprehensive Planning" and well educated and organized Professional Public Administrators, but there were few, if any ready to take on such task to be between Politicians "Bullshit Artist" Business that represents special interest, and Citizens Social Wants that think the Government should do everything...

I talked with and even shared a 25 page "Comprehensive Plan" that could go a long way in these efforts to decentralize; however, the Economic Development and Trade Minister was replaced by someone less focused and in my opinion far less understanding of such policies.

Yet, the Separatist began taking the Airport in Donetsk — scrapping and looting the ½ billion dollar economic hub of the region... The new Ukrainian Government sent in the Army to try to secure the airport that turned into a long-term back and forth fight that latterly scrapped the ½ billion dollar airport along with the economic hub of Donetsk Region...

In addition to experienced "De-escalation and Decentralization" concepts, the sharing of well written "Comprehensive Planning" templates that presented an easy to follow step by step for Decentralization Reforms was never promoted. Such plans could have offered a clear road map for Public-Private-Partnerships, Civil Society Participation with Government... Such Comprehensive Planning is key to any Professional Public Administration and real Reforms...

I went further by offering negotiation frameworks to key Ukrainian negotiators prior to and during the Minsk I and II Agreement process. I even offered possible solutions for Minsk III via a "Crimean Compromise"...

The "Crimean Compromise" would have a key focus on backing the fighting forces back; thereby, creating a "Green zone" to allow OSCE Inspectors to monitor and reduce conflict in Ukraine...

NOTE: (Similar situations will ultimately be needed in Syria, as will a "Divide Syria" and perhaps even parts of Iraq via "Pizza Politics," but this is going to take Men or Women of great resolve that focus on peace and not so much profiteering)...

I encouraged the UN to ask Assad to step down and call for elections... At that time; before the violence, I really felt that Assad could step down and win the Presidency in Syria, and open up a constructive Democracy... But his demonic dictatorship mentality prevented reason and rational thinking that served his citizens best interest...

Gadhafi could have also in Libya; however, the Dictator mind is that of force instead of governmental foundations that give people a voice... Yanukovych had even less difficulties to deal with, he simply had to look at Trade and Economic reforms... But, all three Gadhafi, Assad and Yanukovych chose Mass Murder as opposed to constructive leadership and/or simple professional public administration...

The "Dictator Mindset" was clear with Gadhafi and Assad and it was evident that they were never going to step down. Nor would either ever call for elections to give people a voice, but the United Nations should have tried harder...

Perhaps snap elections could have resulted in preventing civil conflict, and by stepping down opened up the possibility of being elected to power. We have seen successful Politicians stay in power for decades because they listened to their constituent's voices and/or made their constituents believe they were listening…

6
RUSSIA HAS SUPPORTED MASS MURDERS IN BOTH SYRIA AND UKRAINE

Failures at the United Nations led to Russia supporting Mass Murders in both Syria and Ukraine... This is an obvious failure of not only the United Nations, but also Personal and failures for Humanity...

The United Nations must-try to change this mindset--neither Putin/Medvedev, nor "any" United Nations member should be allowed to support Mass Murder.

The World clearly sees where it leads. Russia's support Mass Murders in both Syria and in Ukraine, and ignored Gadhafi's massacre to justify Russia's' UN Security Councils VETO against Syrian Humanitarian Intervention.

If a clearer case for Humanity been presented, and Russia had been a more constructive United Nations partners focusing on Diplomacy and constructive solutions in Syria we would not see Civil Conflict, the vast death, fleeing and rise of terrorism we see today...

The Russian United Nations Security Council VETO against Syrian Humanitarian Intervention led to major civil conflict in Syria that cost more than 350,000 lives, and over 4.5 million refugees fleeing the war zone cold homeless and hungry, as well as a vast increase in Terrorism that we are now seeing in the Middle East, France, and from Africa, to include the recent downing of passenger jet full of Russian civilians...

So I ask the world and Russia "Was my Intervention so bad in Libya?" Absolutely, it100% it was constructive, with a few flaws; however, it is far from the failures that were created in Syrian policy, and the United Nations and certainly Russia should be assumed for creating such death and destruction...

I will mention more on this in a moment; however, it is clear that the United Nations must come together to deal with constructive solutions in Syria, build Safe-Zones, build housing, and economic regions that honor the dignity of humanity and reduce the thoughts of those people becoming martyrs/monsters?

7

GRAND COALITION INTERVENTION TO REDUCE TERRORISM IN SYRIA IS NOT WELL THOUGHT OUT

The rise of Terrorism in the Middle East, Africa, the Paris France attacks have led to anger and calls for a "Grand Coalition" against Terrorism that targets Syria... All are the effectiveness of the 1st Gulf War (which I will discuss my involvements in that success in a moment); however, I do not agree that a "Grand Coalition" is the solution and end all to the problem of Terrorism and/or the Syrian Civil War...

Most Politicians are citing my 1st Gulf War (yes, I helped to plan and organize that also, which gave Saddam 6 months to back out of Kuwait and in the process built the largest multinational coalition in history to kick Saddam out of Kuwait... The first Gulf War was over in 100 hours (4 days, 4 hours, not the dilly dallying around in the desert for a decade like the W Bush return to Iraq.) In fact, I opposed a return to Iraq, and voiced this to Bush prior to and after being elected. See Bush letters.).

A grand "Coalition" is not enough; in reality it only creates more death and destruction... Yet, simple feeding and trying to supply people's needs fleeing Syria is difficult also, and tasking the Military to do this will surely have problems...

Being consistent and focused is worth the hard work... We saw problems in Somalia with my simple Missionary Mission to feed starving Somalis that got converted into a Military Mission by our common-defense not using commonsense, hence "Black Hawk Down."

Seriously folks, you know the military is clueless when a simple chow line to feed people gets 3,000 people killed in a single day. If we continue to allow Proxy control of the Military to lead Civil Society we will continue to get such results...

To quote one of my old professors "Civil Society must control the Military." Yet, I will go one step closer to say that it must have constructive leadership control that advances humanity, focusing on growth and development as opposed to death and destruction...

8
DIPLOMACY AND STATECRAFT

The following chapter was inspired by a reply to Steven A. Cook's perspective in his article for the Council of Foreign Relations.

RE: http://www.cfr.org/diplomacy-and-statecraft/fears-fraying-us-turkey-ties/p31687?cid=soc-Facebook-in-Fears_of_fraying_US_Turkey_Ties-102113

Reading this reminds me of an ungrateful wife, who is not happy with nothing, a man can do...

Personally, I'm happy with the U.S. Turkey Relationship, and would like to counter his argument that we have seen over and over via an American Common Defense that has lost its commonsense... Thus leading America to the current decline in nearly all sectors of the American way of life...

I feel that we have developed stronger ties with Turkey in three ways; Regional Diplomacy, Defense Readiness, and Trade and Commerce...

Regional Diplomacy--Turkey has been side by side with the United States, assisting in dozens of ways to include facilitating talks and fostering Diplomacy. They have also played a part in hosting hundreds of thousands of War Immigrants, helping fund the feeding and caring of those refugees...

In addition, to Humanitarian Assistance, they have been a viable part in echoing to the World pleading the case for the near two million refugees that have fled Syria...

Without Turkey's cooperation and vast intelligence sharing with the U.S., NATO and the United Nations the death and destruction, the refugees and now the Chemical issues would not be in the public's eye...

***NATO/UN Defense Readiness*--**A number of Classified Land, Sea and Air Support in conjunction with the United States is at the ready... They have been ready from Day one as a matter of fact... If the U.S./United Nations Security Council had given authorization for Humanitarian Intervention as they did for my suggestions in Libya then Turkey would have been one of the Primary launching points for such actions...

While conflict is not popular in Turkey or anywhere else in the World I think great commendations should be given to the Turkish leadership for what they have accomplished in supporting United Nations Agreements...

Russian, China support was not given as it was in Libya, we now know and realize via President Obama's speech at the United Nations that they failed to provide leadership that resulted in over 350,000 dead, and four million refugees.

President Obama also pointed out as I have over the past that without the U.S., U.N., and NATO "Humanitarian Intervention" in Libya it would be in the middle of a Civil War today under much of the same state of war we see Syria, with Gadhafi trying to Kill his way back to power...

Currently, the opposition controls the Northern Part of Syria from the Turkish border to the Highway from Baghdad to Aleppo... NOTE: Sadly, with the shift of Secretary of States and continued lack of focus on Syria this area has fractured into ISIS/ISIL hubs...

The highway from Baghdad to the Syrian Coast could have and should become a Dividing GREEN ZONE in Syria to end the war. The *"Syrian Super Highway"* should act as a Toll/Check

Point to foster security and Green Zones...

Trade and Commerce--Turkey like the United States stand to gain far more from Peace than War in the Region... As we know war drains both blood and treasure from our societies. Peace within the region opens up vast trade and commerce opportunities and Turkey being the Bridge from Europe... Of course the United States stands to continue trade and commerce in the region, as well as Defense/Security Agreements as the United States has spent nearly 1/2 Trillion a year in the Middle East for over a Decade.

While this declines and Trade and Commerce Markets open up under the protections of SOFA Agreements and Trade Deals that can vastly improve the Economic Statecraft of the United States... Turkey's relationship with the Region, the United States and the World is much stronger due to the cooperation with the United States...

Turkey is stronger for its Regional Diplomacy that helped the United Nations was in a position to dismantle the Syrian Chemical Stockpile, and possibly end the war in the future.

Turkey's Defense Readiness has been a key partners to enable President Obama to be able to make credible threats against Al Assad of Syria; and lastly Turkey is the bridge between Europe and the Middle East for and Trade and Commerce, which can strengthen and foster political norms.

9
ASSAD CROSSED THE CHEMICAL "RED LINE" I CALL FOR AN ICC-INDICTMENT OF ASSAD; AND PRESIDENT OBAMA TO CALL FOR INTERNATIONAL INTERVENTION

Killing "Peaceful Protesters" and indiscriminately bombing Syrian Cities should have been enough to get an International Criminal Court (ICC) Indictment, but surly the crossing of the Red Line that killed 1,500 men, women and 500 children should have gotten an indictment of Assad.

I encouraged not only President Obama to take action, but also for the establishment of an International Tribunal for the Prosecution of Persons Responsible for Serious Violations of International Humanitarian Law Committed in the Territory of Syria since 2011, more commonly referred to as the International Criminal Tribunal for Syria or ICTS.

ICTS, is a body of the United Nations to be established to prosecute serious crimes committed during the Civil Wars in Syria. The tribunal should be an ad hoc court Established by the United Nations, to be located in The Hague, the Netherlands.

The Court established by Resolution of the United Nations Security Council, should have jurisdiction over the following five clusters of crimes committed in, about, and including those fleeing the territory of the Syria since the beginning of the Civil War in Syria:

1) Abuse of Power,
2) Grave breaches of the Geneva Conventions,
3) Violations of the laws or customs of war,
4) Genocide,
5) and crimes against humanity.

The maximum sentence it can impose should not be less than life imprisonment, and/or the Death Penalty. Various countries have showed a willingness to sign onto such agreements with the UN to carry out custodial sentences.

The final indictments should have been handed down "Immediately". The Tribunal should have had aims to complete all trials by the end of 2014 and/or amended date, and all appeals by 2015 and/or amended date, with the exception of Bashar al-Assad whose trial is expected to end in 2014 along with those responsible for the use of Chemical Weapons in Syria and/or crimes heretofore mentioned...

The United Nations Security Council should have handed down an indictment to allow the United Nations to provide "Humanitarian Intervention" much like "my suggestions for Humanitarian Intervention" that was prosecuted in Libya to prevent mass death and destruction from Muammar Gadhafi.

(NOTE: The United Nations post Libyan Intervention has reservations of conducting like operations in Syria; however, hindsight 20/20 now sees that the Humanitarian Crises is 200 fold that of the Humanitarian War Immigration that occurred in Libya, as well as the vast death and destruction perpetrated by the Syrian Regime.)

I encouraged the US/ UN to call upon the Tribunal HAND DOWN INDICTMENTS IMMEDIATELY; and then finish its work by 31 December 2014 to prepare for its closure and transfer of its responsibilities to the International Residual Mechanism for Criminal Tribunals which will begin functioning for the ICTS branch on 1 July 2015 and/or amended date, but there was no Indictment...

The Tribunal could have completed all outstanding first instance trials, including those of Bashar al-Assad and other handed down within the indictment. It could have conducted completed all appeal proceedings for which the notice of appeal against the judgment or sentence is filed before 1 July 2014 and/or amended date. Any appeals could have been handled by the Residual Mechanism. Sadly, there was no indictment...

President Obama begins to take action--After Al Assad of Syria allegedly cross the Chemical Weapons "Red Line" I wrote the U.S. Ambassador to the United Nations and the U.S. Mission to the United Nations and made a number of suggestions such as begin discussions at the U.N for a possible Multi-National Coalition against Syria as well as suggesting President Obama should address Congress to authorize presenting the Indictment of the Assad Regime to the United Nations to seek justification for "Humanitarian Intervention" in Syria.

I advised that President Obama should recognize that 1) in the past he supported Congressional Approval before any intervention that is not an eminent threat to the United States. 2) America and the International Community has a Responsibility not to turn a blind eye to the Indictable Offenses of Crimes Against Humanity by the Assad Regime, and 3) lastly, 3) MILITARY "HUMANITARIAN INTERVENTION" STRATEGY...

1) In the past he supported Congressional Approval before any intervention that is not an eminent threat to the United States.

a) I think as a Senator that understands Constitutional Authority is reasonable to seek Constitutional Approval for any military intervention that may not be of eminent threat to America. "Reputation and Credibility" played a huge part in this as the more talk, the more serious the situation became. It ultimately brought Russia and Iran to the Table to assist in negotiating the destruction of the Syrian Chemical Weapons as well as Iran negotiating a Non-Nuclear Agreements.

b) Yet, as President there are Global responsibilities that require a President to be able to reach out and deal with Crimes against Humanity to protect those that cannot protect themselves.

c) These are noteworthy and justifiable causes that reach the core of American Constitutional Principles and the Core Morality of Humanity...

2) America and the International Community has a Responsibility not to turn a blind eye to the Indictable Offenses of Crimes against Humanity by the Assad Regime, and

a) America and Friends of America from around the World have been drafting "Indictable Offenses" to present to the United Nations.

b) These "Indictable Offenses" presented to the United Nations will ask to convene an "International Criminal Tribunal for Syria (ICTS).

c) The ICTS should indict based on a number of sub issues related to Abuse of Power, Grave breaches of the Geneva Conventions, Violations of the laws or customs of war, Genocide, and crimes against humanity.

3) MILITARY "HUMANITARIAN INTERVENTION" STRATEGY... We propose to seek Congressional Approval for the following, but not limited to

a) Imposing a "No Fly Zone". Enforce that no fly zone via "Classified Drone Radar Systems" as eyes in the sky to detect flight activities by the al-Assad Regime.

b) Criss-Cross unmanned Drone's across Syria to take out Syrian Military Aircraft and Massive Tank/Artillery, SAM positions via drones, air support and naval operations.

c) Neighboring Countries patrol and encroach upon Syrian Airspace.

d) PSYOPS maintain Talking Points to clearly indicate that al-Assad has been indicted by the International Criminal Tribunal for Syria (ICTS).

e) Train Syrian Opposition to prepare to take the Syrian Capital.

I continue to believe in seeking Congressional Approval for Military Action that is not a direct eminent threat to America, note that America and the International Community has a moral responsibility to not turn a blind eye to Indictable Offense of Crimes Against Humanity, and seek Military "Humanitarian Intervention" with strategy that makes it clear to the Assad Regime that the International Community has been appalled at his actions and the abuse of his power, the treatment of his people and the committing of war crimes...

War Crimes Feelings and Talking points --I grew up in a time when America stood for Freedom, Truth and Justice, and I also learned that you should lead by example...

In the case of Syria we either lead or we turn off our TV's and turn our backs on the millions of helpless men, women and children that are being brutalized; thereby, allowing the Assad Regime to lead his Dictatorial Death March into a more brutal world of the future...

I for one would not want to be in the Boots of a Dictator that has brought Dishonor upon himself and for his Country. I like most Americans believe in Freedom, Truth and Justice and we can clearly see that Syrians are not free to live their lives in Peace.

It takes very little imagination after seeing the chemical weapons brutality to ponder the thought of families saying their nightly prayers, and nervously putting their children to bed... Perhaps closing the window to deafen the sound of the Assad shelling in the streets, perhaps even a bit of inner prayers that the shelling would not get closer. Then perhaps turn on the Air Conditioner to block out even more sounds of war. Then a kiss goodnight and telling of the child not to play his games on his phone or pad too long that rest is important...

Then just as the family begins to fall asleep the deadly chemical begin to fill the rooms, and their lungs, waking, coughing, choking and grasping for air and life...

Yet, a few blocks away the Assad's were fast asleep in their heavily guarded Palace. He rested well even though he had already been responsible for over two million refugees, one million of which are children, and over 100,000 deaths, mostly innocent Civilians from indiscriminate attacks on

Syrian Cities... So, what are a few more lives to him, he want lose any sleep...

People like me, and other Americans and true Citizens of the World lose sleep worrying about the Assad brutality, death and destruction, the millions of starving, cold and wet refugees, which are the lucky ones, which managed to escape death... We also worry about the instability of the region, the lack of real leadership, statesmen that bring growth and development to the region along with peace...

Yet, Assad is not a Statement with the values of Democracy, he is a Dictator clinging to power and his leadership is that of death of then nearly half the amount of now over 350,000 of his own citizens, four million starving and cold refugees... This alone should have been enough for the International Community to act; however, Humanity has had a laps in leadership, but now it is time to regain our Humanity, and end conflict in Syria...

Evidence and Strategy Talking points for the prosecution of the International Criminal Tribunal for Syria (ICTS) to justify United Nations "Humanitarian Intervention" actions by the International Community... NOTE: The President should make his Case to Congress, then agree with Congress that he is to take his Case to the United Nations to call for action...

1) Abuse of Power,

al-Assad is not an Elected Official; yet, he has held power in Syria against the will of the people of Syria for decades.

Unlike Egypt that have had elections, street protest elections, and now even have a third round of planned Elections to be held within the year to honor the Wishes of the Egyptian people; al-Assad on the other hand refuses to hold elections in order to maintain Dictatorship power via military strong-arming, and destroying any and all Syrian Citizens who oppose him... Eye Witness Accounts/Documented Evidence from those that have fled Syria.

2) Grave breaches of the Geneva Conventions,

Grave breaches of the Rule of International Law, i.e. those rules of law within the Geneva Convention guidance to avoid inhuman acts of war...

Eye Witness Account and Documented Evidence from those that have fled Syria.

3) Violations of the laws or customs of war,

A war crime is a serious violation of the laws applicable in armed conflict (also known as international humanitarian law) giving rise to individual criminal responsibility.

Eye Witness Accounts/Documented Evidence from those that have fled Syria.

Examples of war crimes include "murder, the ill-treatment or deportation of civilian residents of an occupied territory to slave labor camps," "the murder or ill-treatment of prisoners of war," the killing of prisoners, "the wanton destruction of cities, towns and villages, and any devastation not justified by military, or civilian necessity."

Eye Witness Accounts and Documented Evidence from those that have fled Syria.

Similar concepts, such as perfidy, have existed for many centuries as customs between civilized countries, but these customs were first codified as international law in the Hague Conventions of 1899 and 1907.

The modern concept of a war crime was further developed under the auspices of the Nuremberg Trials based on the definition in the London Charter that was published on August 8, 1945. (Also see Nuremberg Principles.)

Along with war crimes the charter also defined crimes against peace and crimes against humanity, which are often committed during wars and in concert with war crimes.

4) Genocide,

al-Assad's bombarding of innocent unarmed civilians in areas that would appose him, has led to over 2 Million war refugees fleeing Syria and the International Community in conjunction with Syria's neighboring countries to care and feed those that al-Assad has sought to destroy...

Eye Witness Accounts/Documented Evidence from those that have fled Syria.

NOTE: 2 million leaving the country or facing death is a pretty darn good bit of evidence for this...
al-Assad has forced out over 2 Million Syrians, and systematically erased a number of small cities from existence as they fled the conflict, as well as destroying fleeing unarmed men, women and children while fleeing unarmed...

Article 22 of The Hague IV ("Laws of War: Laws and Customs of War on Land (Hague IV); October 18, 1907") states that "The right of belligerents to adopt means of injuring the enemy is not unlimited"

Over the last century many other treaties have introduced positive laws that place constraints on belligerents (see International treaties on the laws of war). Some of the provisions, such as those in The Hague, the Geneva, and Genocide Conventions, are considered to be part of customary international law, and are binding on all.

Others are only binding on individuals if the belligerent power to which they belong is a party to the treaty which introduced the constraint.

5) and crimes against humanity.

al-Assad has used his power to oppress and destroy his own citizens by spray over 3,000 with Nero-Toxin's and killed nearly 1,500 innocent unarmed men, women and children; thereby, treating innocent Syrians as insects as opposed to human beings...

Eye Witness Accounts and Documented Evidence from those that have been involved and the United Nations Weapons Inspectors.

Crimes against humanity, as defined by the Rome Statute of the International Criminal Court Explanatory Memorandum, "are particularly odious offenses in that they constitute a serious attack on human dignity or grave humiliation or a degradation of human beings."

They are not isolated or sporadic events, but are part either of a government policy (although the perpetrators need not identify themselves with this policy) or of a wide practice of atrocities tolerated or condoned by a government or a de facto authority.

Murder; extermination; torture; rape; political, racial, or religious persecution and other inhumane acts reach the threshold of crimes against humanity only if they are part of a widespread or systematic practice.
Eye Witness Accounts/Documented Evidence from those that have fled Syria.

Isolated inhumane acts of this nature may constitute grave infringements of human rights, or depending on the circumstances, war crimes, but may fall short of falling into the category of crimes under discussion."
Eye Witness Accounts/Documented Evidence from those that have fled Syria.

MILITARY "HUMANITARIAN INTERVENTION" STRATEGY...

a) Impose a "No Fly Zone". Enforce that no fly zone via "Classified Drone Radar Systems" as eyes in the sky to detect flight activities by the al-Assad Regime.

b) Criss Cross unmanned Drone's across Syria to take out Syrian Military Aircraft and Massive Tank/Artillery, SAM positions via drones, air support and naval operations.

c) Neighboring Countries patrol and encroach upon Syrian Airspace.

d) PSYOPS maintain Talking Points to clearly indicate that al-Assad has been indicted by the International Criminal Tribunal for Syria (ICTS).

e) Train Syrian Opposition to prepare to take the Syrian Capital.

10
SYRIAN CHEMICAL WEAPONS DESTRUCTION
THE
MISSED OPPORTUNITY
TO STOP THE SYRIAN CIVIL WAR

We missed a great opportunity to stop the Civil War in Syria when the International Community built the Billion Dollar Chemical Weapons burn facility... At that time I felt5 a simple three fold plan cold work; 1) End the war, 2) Turn over the Syrian Finances to the United Nations to find in-kind funds, and 3) follow a United Nations "Comprehensive Planning" mandate to spur growth and development in increase Gross Domestic Production (GDP).

***Ending the War in Syria*--** via some type of political settlement such as "Dividing Syria" into regions, which were under control by constructive opposition forces at that time.

Such territorial control would have been the most reasonable. That solution could have either broke-up Syria, or politically cut it up in Congressional Regions; thereby, allowing "Power Sharing"... Ending the war allowing United Nations money to be used for the destruction of WMD's and to the Government funds to better Syrians daily lives...

Syria could have turned over Financial Management to the United Nations, the IMF-- and other such organizations that have financial backgrounds like me that can quickly make recommendations that could vastly improve Syria's Financial Condition...

A better financial situation will allow a number of State Owned Enterprises to contribute to the efforts of destroying Syrian WMD's that were posing international threats. Post WMD destruction could have brought Peace and Prosperity to Syria... *A United Nations Global Reform Mandate via "Comprehensive Planning"* https://docs.google.com/viewer?a=v& pid=explorer&chrome=true&srcid=0B- ygIxNdW7E9YWE5NTBmNjMtZmY5O C00YmMyLThkNmUtNTc1MWJhMDV hM2Zj&hl=en_US

A mandate would allow a form of Democracy via Citizen affecting the Local, Regional and State Levels. Comprehensive Planning via a UN Mandate would have allowed People to return to Syria and to begin getting their lives back together.

Vast Capital Improvement Projects at these levels can aid in the funding in a number of ways. The Four million people that Assad caused to flee out of Syria and into Refugee Camps were once thriving families that paid taxes and contributed to the improvement of Syria.

The Syrian people would surely like to revitalize Syria post conflict and be a contributor as opposed to living on the mercy of hand-outs from the International Community...

Now it will take years to build Safe-Zones and to rebuild the required housing to meet refugee's needs... Yet, the reluctance of the International Community to accept Syrian's due to the threat of Refugee Terrorist more hardships will fall upon the Syrians refugees...

A quality written United Nations "Comprehensive Planning" Mandate would allow a form of Democracy via Citizen affecting the Local, Regional and State Levels. Yet, it will take a long term commitment to do this...

I think we will see vast housing developments to try to bring Syrians back as part of UNDP "Comprehensive Planning."

11
$ 1 BILLION SPENT TO DESTROY CHEMICAL WEAPONS, THE RISE OF ISIL AND ISIS VS CLINTONS OPPOSITION THAT WAS IN CONTROL OF THE NORTH OF SYRIA

I really hate to be negative, but the Kerry/Lavrov meeting has a lot of flaws and impractical aspects...

Okay, back to step one; after the Kerry/Lavrov meeting in Geneva, Switzerland to place the Syrian Chemical Weapons under the United Nation's Control... As I said from day one a "Case for Indictment" of Assad must be made at the United Nations Security Council under Chapter 7 of the United Nations Organizational Charter http://www.un.org/en/documents/ch arter/chapter7.shtml ... I think there is a Case and the Agreement today will be impossible to do in the middle of a Civil War...

Secondly, the NBC (Nuclear Biological Chemical) weapons free zone in the Middle East is a step forward, but getting others on board and taking Iran's Nuclear Program and placing it under the United Nations will also be tough as it will appear that the U.S. is not honoring agreements as Assad fails on a deal that he can't deliver during a Civil War...

Thirdly, while it makes for good political TV sadly a real solution for stopping the war was not offered... Only an end to the Civil War could solve the problem. I wrote before that a possible breakup/"Divide Syria" as a possible Solution.

Kerry~ "This is not a time for Armchair Isolationism." Okay, nice statement, and I had also suggested like statements during the buildup of the 1st Gulf War, but what is his point?

I would love to give a lecture on "Runaway Internationalism" and how the lack of quality management of "Internationalism related to Free Trade vs Fair Trade has America in a 1 Trillion a year Imbalance" and how that has vastly affected America's Economic/National Security Interest. But, that is not the real topic of discussion. This discussion is about the Use of Force in Syria "Might is Right" vs "Right is Might"...

During the 1st Gulf War there was a huge part of Americans that felt that we should just mind our own business and stay out of the Middle East/Iraq. While I saw it as a clear expansion of a Tyrannical Dictator that threatened the Global Economy as he took over Kuwait which was the Gas Station to the World and Wall Street was the Cashier...

Today, Americans, British, Russians and others are sick and tired of seeing conflict in the Middle East as am I. I tried to voice my opposition before the George W. Bush return to Iraq that America was being sold a false bill of goods that would cost us trillions of dollars and destabilize the region.

Now America and the rest of the world see it. The Bush return diminished America's integrity, reputation and credibility along with our ability to yield economic statecraft influence. The Bush "Might is Right" policy failed and undermined my concepts, as well what I feel to be the Obama Administrations "Right is Might" policy...

Right is Might has vast responsibility. First and foremost it has to make a case. (writing from the other side of the Planet this "Armchair Internationalist," sees a vast number of International Blunders with U.S. Foreign Policy, Free Trade instead of Fair Trade, Military engagement that has cost America Trillions of Dollars with an added nearly 16Trillion dollars' worth of new debt since 2000 (now over 19 Trillion Dollars) www.usdebtclock.org and a host of other issues).

In the effort to stay on the point of "Right is Might" I have tried to show Policy Makers how to make a simple 5 Point Case for the American People and the United Nations. That Case is that al-Assad should be indicted for:

1) Abuse of Power,
2) Grave breaches of the Geneva Conventions,
3) Violations of the laws or customs of war,
4) Genocide,
5) and crimes against humanity.

The Alternative Option is a "Diplomatic Solution" would be to offer Assad "CONSTITUTIONAL MONARCHY"; thereby, making his family Royalty in Syria, and giving the Syrian people the right to elect a

President/Prime Minister... Yet, there is no way to get to the Diplomatic Solution without proving to the World that "Right is Might" and that we either engage militarily or we stop the Conflict now under Stalemate allowing the "KING" to be protected by Russia and Iran.

Yet, that opens up a national security questions for America and the World, and will lead to a Nuclear Arms Race in the Middle East if the U.S. caves into the use of Chemical Weapons and Iran's Nuclear Program... THE IRAN NUCLEAR ISSUE HAS BECOME ONE IN THE SAME...

ONLY A "NUCLEAR, BIOLOGICAL AND CHEMICAL FREE MIDDLE EAST POLICY" adheres to the "Right is Might" policy objectives... If not, will we see a near WWIII type event occurs in the Middle East with a host of Arab League nations attack both Syria and Iran to prevent them from going Nuclear? I think so... NOW IS A TIME FOR A VOICE OF REASON TO PREVAIL BEFORE THIS HAPPENS...

Secretary Kerry, President Obama, nor Ambassador Powers or any of the other Administration Talking Heads are getting to the point. Nor are they persuading the American people or the International Community that stepping in is the "Right" thing to do, nor are they communicating the problems of engagement and how it could quickly expand into a WWIII type situation without the International Community supporting an "Indictment" of Assad...

Nor is the United Nations discussing how a couple companies are profiting from the Nuclear Project in Iran that presents the danger of costing millions of lives and creating vast death and destruction... They are clueless to the heated tensions and long term political aspects and history of the region... This minor energy interest stands to engulf the region into flames...

Diplomacy has become like the blundering Bush policies of "Might over Right" issue that has other International actors such as Iran, and Russia supporting a regime that used Chemical Weapons that killed about 1,500 people. Nearly 500 were innocent little children... This is absolutely crazy to be supporting a regime that would do such a thing...

The simple question that all "Armchair Isolationist" should be asking "Is Might Right" in this case... If any leader in the World today has any integrity, decency and simple respect for Humanity then the answer should be "NO, Might is not Right" in the Chemical attack in Syria, nor are the other 5 points mentioned above.

The entire world should be condemning the attack along with the

100,000 he lives he has cost (most of which were indiscriminate bombings of Cities within Syria), which caused nearly 5 million to be displaced within Syria and 2 million War Immigrants that have fled into neighboring countries... 1 Million of which are Children that are cold, hungry and traumatized by war... We cannot begin to imagine what the millions of children are enduring within Syria without getting a bit overwhelmed with emotion...

Syrian Olighargdom and American Foreign Policy is are both flawed... Without keeping it simple and looking at "Right is Might" and convincing the American People and the World at the United Nations with solid evidence then our Military Might will not be looked at as being the right thing to do...

12
ASSAD NOT THE WORD OF GOD

I highly doubt Al Assad represents the word of God in Syria after such Devilish Deeds of death and destruction over the past two years that he unleashed upon unarmed innocent civilians within Syrian Cities that we all have been witness to...

Al Assad's televised captive special interest arena audience vs hundreds of thousands in multiple Refugee Camps that could fill the arena hundreds of times over are just crying out to be heard... Where is the leadership that will speak and give hope to those camps? Where is the opposition to show the world that they too can fill grand halls many times over with Anti-Al Assad voices...

Over two years ago, I saw Syrian President Al Assad give a Pep-Rally address to a room full of cheering people as he did again Sunday, January 06, 2013... He basically, said the same thing then as now; blaming external conspiracies as opposed to accepting that his internal Dictatorial policies have failed...

While the world debates Al Assad's attempt to spin his olive branch speech while having his military destroy the lives of anyone willing to question him... He and his special interest supporters are making their last ditch effort to cling to their dominating power over the military force, while the innocent hundreds of thousands of refugees have no voice...

I think Russia and China clearly see this and are beginning to back away from his support. Iran will most likely continue to support as they have a great kinship in his policies that are not far from Dictatorial as the Supreme Religious Leader is a Dictator in disguise...

The hundreds of thousands of Syrian War Refugees that could fill the speech hall more than 200 times had a voice, I am sure that they would share their anger for much more than simple Democracy and the wanting of a Constitutional Vote, and a Representative Voice over that of the Al Assad Dictatorship… They would share the stories of their once hopes and dreams and the sadness of seeing those hopes and dreams diminish due to the Devilish deeds of Al Assad…

Their heart felt talking points would be that of being directly in the middle of more than Sixty Thousand dead and how their families, loved ones and friends' hopes and dreams were destroyed by Al Assad's' directed Air, Tank and Mortar attacks on their civilian cities in a forceful attempt to maintain a dying Devilish Dictatorial regime…

The Opposition Leadership has called hundreds, if not thousands of group meetings within the camps, and the Opposition Leadership has heard the horrific stories, and can honestly and justly stand in front of the world and before God and be a voice calling for change...

The International Media has to do little more than go to the War Refugee camps and listen to the rising voices for groups of thousands, tens of thousands, hundreds of thousands and ultimately the millions of Syrians that are calling for an end to the death and devastation from the Al Assad regime...

Why should the Al Assad regime get a voice while the Opposition voices are silenced... The World needs to see the Opposition groups, which are becoming the voices of the Syrian people that are crying out to the world in horrific conditions as they have barely escaped the death, and devastation of the Al

Assad regime; yet, now living inhumane conditions...

I highly doubt Al Assad is the voice of God for his country; as Al Assad vowed his enemies would go to Hell... It is God to judge and not for man to judge who is worthy or unworthy to be plunged into the depths of Hell...

I do not claim to know the mind of God; however, a reasonable God-fearing person would think that God is more apt to listen to the hundreds of thousands of children, and families that Al Assad has put in Hell like conditions during his regime, and more especially over the past two years of war...

I am sure that God, along with the world has watched over the past two years as Al Assad clung to power by committing War Crimes that targeted, and destroyed cities full of unarmed innocent citizens. Civilians that littered the streets with the bodies of innocent women, and children, which were incapable of defending themselves ...

I am sure that God has saw, as the world has saw the Dictators rampage of death and destruction of his nation and the innocent with total disregard for human rights ...

Those of us that have followed this over the past two years could imagine that God has heard the minute-by-minute, hour-by-hour, day-by-day, week-by-week, month-by-month, and now year-by-year pleas, cries and prayers for the Dictator and his Devilish devastation upon his cities full of innocent old men, women and children...

Therefore, if anyone will be plunged into Hell, it will be Al Assad for the cruelty that he has unleashed upon the citizens of Syria under for their hopes and prayed for a better quality of life...

I do not subscribe to "Death Democracy" and have a huge problem of supporting war over Diplomacy; however, I suggested "Humanitarian Intervention" in Libya as I felt it was justified in preventing the mass destruction of multiple cities and vast loss of civilian lives…

United Nations discussions of Syrian "Humanitarian Intervention" became debated by the U.S, Russia and China that offered little in the way of early Diplomatic efforts to encourage Constitutional Reforms, the stepping down and/or a new Constructional Declaration of the Syrian People to give Al Assad "Monarchy" status and/or the opportunity to run for President…

Diplomacy failed and the Al Assad regime chose the sward over the pen and a bill of rights for his citizens to ease his Dictatorial oppression… We have passed through the Cross Road where the deal with the Devil is often done and now the end may be the anger left behind from the tens of thousands of innocent souls sweeping him Al Assad away to be thrown into the lake of fire to collect his soulless body...

My only sadness is of his wife and family; however, deep down she might have pondered the fact that she was marrying a Dictator, and not a man that would value her voice and/or the voice of the Syrian people...

I respect and value the great attention that American Secretary of State Secretary Hillary Clinton, as well as Ambassador Susan Rice has giving to try to prevent "Civil War" in Syria... I am also proud of their efforts in working with global partners, which has led to Iran accepting the U.N./IAEA Weapons Inspectors into Iran to prevent War...

Secretary Clinton and Ambassador Rice have a tough job at times. They have rarely grandstanded; in fact, they have taken a back seat to the Arab League and other regional Geopolitical participants, and allowed them to try to come to a regional solution to prevent "Civil War" within Syria...

From day one, I tried to be a voice of reason and have favored "Diplomatic Delegations." I even went against many of our American Diplomats and asked that Assad have a chance to be proactive and constructive... I strongly believed that Assad, which was respected and supported by a great number of his citizens, as was Gadhafi in Libya, would not go down the same destructive paths...

I am a political junkie with a fairly vast track record in making constructive suggestions that has benefited humanity... I perhaps set my hopes too high in President Assad.

The Russian monitors believed in Assad leadership as well; however, Assad has also let them down and has offered nothing to prove to Russia, myself or the World that is watching the violence escalate that he is in any way, shape or form being proactive and/or constructive in preventing violence in his country.

Assad has held firm and maintained his blame game accusations that America and the West is responsible for his failed leadership... Assad failed in the faith that I put in his leadership abilities and he failed Russia and the World, just as he failed his citizens... Assad has clearly chosen violence, as opposed to welcoming assistance and the call for Elections by the Arab League to allow the people to decide and to give them a real voice...

Russian Diplomats have publically stated that a U.N. Resolution for President Assad to step down would resort into Syria going into a "Civil War"... I do not think that there is any denying that any Russia Ambassador monitoring the situation in Syria would not recognize that Syria is already in a "Civil War"... I think that the Arab League, Human Rights organizations that have been monitoring the citation would deny that Syria has already fallen into "Civil War"...

I think we all clearly see that Assad chose internal violence over that of simple reforms. Assad did not welcome citizen involvement in the policymaking process and chose oppression over participation...

Leadership should always recognize this basic "Universal Human Right" of citizens to peacefully voice their concerns... I think it is a no brainer that Peaceful citizens should not be ran down the same streets that their taxpaying funds pay for either, while just trying to voice themselves...

President Assad chose violence over reforms and peace in his country… Assad has held firm in playing the blame game over "Diplomatic Delegations" which have tried to help him and the citizens of his nation in a constructive way… This has created vast hardships on the Syrian people and the World does not like to see such cruelty and lack of disregard for peaceful citizens trying to voice their selves.

I see no other way to deal with the "Civil War" situation in Syria other than to ask him to step down, and have elections… I agree with the Arab League that this will stop the violence and allow citizens to rise up, and have a say within their government… Perhaps Assad is still popular enough to be elected President, but there will be a great many others elected that will represent the citizens many concerns…

The other path is all out "Civil War" and the Russians will surely Veto any U.N. Resolution that will give the opposition the ability to engage in a "Fair Fight"…

Assad's regime has purchased billions of dollars' worth of Arms from Russia over the years; however, "Darwinism where the strongest survives, over that of Democracy" would be an injustice in the eyes of the United Nations and the World…

13
BRIAN SAYERS THE NEW "LORD OF WAR"

One has to wonder if perhaps Brian Sayers started out with some sort of conscious or cause, but eventually turned cold, or are they became the instruments of failed Diplomacy?

I being more of a Diplomatic Analyst always looking to prevent conflict than to participate in one...

Yet, have found myself involved in a number of Wars and Crises Management situations in the past, in Panama, the 1st Gulf war in Iraq, in Somalia, the initial stages of Bosnia demanding and entry and exit strategy, and more recently suggesting "Humanitarian Intervention" and a "Divide Libya Policy" that I felt would prevent Civil Conflict in Libya...

I do not like war and certainly do not see myself as a "Weapons Dealer" without a conscious; yet, one has to question one's self from time to time, and ponder if one felt strongly enough would he become such a person?

Lucky for me I do not have to answer that question, for there is someone out there now taking the lead in Syria by the name of Brian Sayers.

CNN International reported that the United States has authorized an American based group to provide financial assistance and provide more weaponry to the Syrian resistance.

Brian Sayers, of the , claims to have obtained a waiver from the United States Treasury Department Office of Foreign Asset Control (OFAC) last week; however, the document is no longer at the link identified above…

Brian Sayers made a number of claims after. He like most of us got tired of watching kids become casualties of war. In addition to financial support, which he intends to use to purchase and supply weapons he also conducts Google Earth type battle reports and shares with the "Free Syrian Army"...

Sayers, of the Washington, D.C. area is not lacking in experience. Among his claims are that of working with NATO operations in Brussels before seeking to help the Syrian Support Group in Washington.

Sayers also stated that he requires his FSA military command to sign onto the "Geneva Conventions—Laws of War" as well as other commitment to democracy and the freedoms that come with it...

I sent Mr. Sayers an email at info@syriansupportgroup.org to thank him for his service; while, pondering why Diplomacy failed to prevent the Civil War in Syria, and ponder why my "Diplomatic Delegation" suggestions to Susan Rice (The United States Ambassador to the United Nations) was not considered. Sadly, we now we have to watch death and destruction daily on our Television sets, read about it in the news and hear about it the streets...

14
(HELP)
HUMANITARIAN ENGINEERED
LABOR PROJECT

"Humanitarian Engineered Labor Projects" (HELP) to build a Wall of Co-Existence Condo-Settlements around Israel, and build "Peace Park" http://thesop.org/story/20120122/peace-park-and-my-two-state-solution-via-the-venus-project.html...

I would like to discuss how my suggestion for the productive AID for the near 2 million "War Immigrants" via my "Humanitarian Engineered Labor Projects" (HELP)...

The key concept of (HELP) is to focus on creating a "Comprehensive War Immigration Plan" to convert War Immigrants into a "Corp of Infrastructure Engineers"... This new Corp of Infrastructure Engineers will maintain refocus the War Immigrants bold revolutionary pride by taking them out of a war zone and give them respect and decency by providing jobs, while allowing the War Immigrants to repay their Host Country, many fold…

(HELP) will be a mutual relationship between the War Immigrants and the Host Country to help each other… War Immigrants will be provided with a bank account, and a job to construct Infrastructure projects in the Host Country. The new Infrastructure Projects can be quickly designed to focus on increasing Growth and Development for the Host Country…

The Host Country must quickly assess their communities and cities to see where War Immigrant labor and expertise can be most valuable to spur future growth and development. Then give presentations and collect ideas, and recruit from the War Immigrants that are able to participant in the (HELP) plans…

This can be done by assessing the area jointly with the War Immigrants and the Host Country Communities and Cities via the following "Comprehensive Plan"... United Nations Global Reform Mandate
https://docs.google.com/viewer?a=v& pid=explorer&chrome=true&srcid=0B-ygIxNdW7E9YWE5NTBmNjMtZmY5O C00YmMyLThkNmUtNTc1MWJhMDV hM2Zj&hl=en_US

(HELP) can be funded via a UN mandate, and host tax dollars... Those projects can be jointly funded via worldwide capital market funds syndicated to develop vast growth projects. (HELP) could increase War Immigrant labor opportunities, as well as spur economic development and investment opportunities to increase jobs, future housing and commercial development, or even trade and commerce at ports in Host Countries...

Small to Large-scale projects such as building ring or short connector roads and railroads around key cities spurs growth and economic development... So does key parks and paver-promenades and plazas... Such projects can revitalize and/or turn eyesore areas into new grand plaza's... Obviously, new ring and rail projects provide many new sites for land development of office, logistics/industrial, apartments, housing communities as well as retail shops...

I feel that we could develop a mass organized War Immigrant worker/labor camp concept where thousands of War Immigrants could be allowed entry to Host Countries via (HELP) focused planning... (HELP) camps will help Host Countries America develop infrastructure projects such as large scale Military/Corps of Engineer projects or the TVA post-Depression days in the United States...

While in the Army, I used to participate in mass mobilization of tens of thousands of troops, and the rail heading of hundreds of tanks across German in just a few short hours... Once there the mission went into effect. Some times that involved establishing temporary housing, and the building of roads, airfields, and so forth... The same type of projects can be done in key areas with War Immigrants and when things are safe they can return with those skills, rebuild, and improve their own country...

Mobile housing can help establish a bit of comfort in a "Hostel/Hotel/Makeshift Barracks" to help facilitate migrant workers in Train Cars, fast makeshift housing, etc. for the more rugged men willing to deploy to key Infrastructure projects...

Such mobile labor movement can add real value by developing Host Country infrastructure projects to spurs growth and development. These mobile work camps would supply reasonable wages in safe and secure surroundings and provide respect and pride for both the Host Country as well as the War Immigrants...

Before, people start thinking this is silly. I remind you that the American Military and the U.S./NATO/U.N. has built mobile cities in Iraq and Afghanistan using Military forces, and contract labor to build infrastructure in those areas today... So, why would it not work in America as well? All while increasing America's GDP, providing new Tax Base Jobs for Immigrant Workers and Americans alike and creating investment opportunities for World Wide Capital Markets...

I dubbed this concept the (HELP) for obvious reasons... A revolution of ideas that focus on spurring large-scale economic development projects throughout Host Countries. (HELP) can focus on retraining War Immigrants to be able to lead new Public Administration Projects when they return to their country to rebuild, and enrich their selves and their country... Reference material:

http://www.un.org/apps/news/story. asp?NewsID=45684&Cr=syria&Cr1=

15
LEADERSHIP

My view of Leadership and how he has managed to influence several Presidents; thereby, saving millions of lives, affecting the economic fate of nations and reducing the threat of weapons of mass destruction...

Okay, the "Thesis Statement" is about long winded, but I promise to make a point that will change your life... Most people only look to the top of the Pyramid to initiate change. Most are are stuck on authority to the point that they rarely question anything, to include asking questions in class. Many in fact, rarely, if ever asked any questions or challenged with debate be it in class and/or their community, state, nation, etc...

Very few people are comfortable at the top. They like to look at the issue hindsight 20/20 and try to hold others accountable rarely for being affective, but more for the simplest failure in leadership, while never offering to be part of that leadership...

Real Leadership welcomes clashes between those that are internal innovators... Yet, more often than not those that claim to be innovators are really clueless to the real direction leadership should be going... That is when real communication and trust becomes the key, and when I am at my best and rise to the occasion...

Real Leadership is willing to recognize those that always look to the Top and those that are thinking and advising at the Top Level... With this thought in mind real leadership is aware that little change can occur if it is driven from the Top...

Listening to the People and/or those that are connected to real people, with real concerns, as well as real experts that have the best intentions for Top Leadership often rise to be change makers... Top down leadership if often that of special interest and few buy into it, and is often a poorly proposed agenda with a real lack of commitment as it is not by the people and for the people's best interest... Business is often the same...

I think most of us that have ever watched the news can realize that more often than not that a President is no more or less than our neighbor, co-worker, friend, fellow civic club, church member, etc...

Like any President they have opinions, often they are just that opinions, not fact, but just there perspective of the way an issue will go and/or not go... In other words, they really don't have a clue in most cases and will often wait till people in support of the issue is a higher percentage than those that appose before they get on board and/or buy-in to the issue...

I on the other hand often think far beyond that... I anticipate the percentages, but often realize that those percentages will be low; however, real leadership can go against the percentages to affect real change... It is hard, but if you have developed trust and confidence as a Policy Maker you might just pull a bottom up shift in the Policy Making process...

Recently I made such suggestions on Syria and Iran with the anticipation that the American Public and the World would be divided; however, the key was to provide constructive leadership to affect change and vastly reduce destructive behavior in Syria.

The focus to destroy their Chemical Weapons; while affecting constructive Table Negotiations with Iran to possibly bring their Peaceful Nuclear Program under the United Nations; thereby, dealing with two of the most serious threats to Humanities future, all while being an unpopular stance... Now that is leadership, and a heck of a lot of sleepless nights...

Many of you might think this is an "Arrogant View of Leadership", but it is really a "Humble View of Leadership"...

We have to look no further than today's headlines of Government-Shut-Down to realize that there is a great divide and vast cynicism in American Policy Making...

I know that the President has a number of Advisors and Special Interest as well I also know that the "Commissioned Congress" that hold the purse strings of Government are also beholden to Special Interest... The debate and confusion that adds to Policy Making only creates gridlock and Presidential Policies of Appeasement...

The rhetoric today is that the President is more willing to talk with Iran than with Congress... Well, that was last week's problem and it is ongoing and a problem that hasn't been able to be solved for over a decade. So, instead of Congress giving the President a bit of Credit, it is now back to criticism and commission politics that will most likely undermine America's best interest again...

So, I will give the President a bit of applause... I think he took the high ground, even though he and I felt he should go to Congress to buy a bit of time for America and Global Good... The Debate brought out those that are real leaders and those that have no backbone to sit in the Chair at the highest levels... We know who they are and they will pay the price in the future when they claim to be leaders...

While many were saying, and trying to capitalize on sayings like "We Have No Dog In That Fight"...

Americans and the World know who were the real leaders, from those want-a-be leaders like Rand Paul, which would turn, tuck their tail between their legs and run away...

Americans also know those that have favored unjust wars; thereby, unleashing the Dogs of War as McConnell has for nearly three decades, since beating Dee Huddleston with the silly Devil Dog TV Adds that put McConnell in control of selling out America to the Chinese...

Ultimately, it was the self-proclaimed Presidential Mutt that stood its ground, and protected America, and faithfully stood for the World's Best interest...

16
FINAL EXPERT OPINION

We need people with a brain far more than more bombs and boots on the ground... I have great concerns for a "Grand Coalition Intervention into Syria to reduce Terrorism like my planning of the 1st Gulf War planning.

I appreciate citing and comparing the need for such planning and organizing of multinational coalition during the 1st Gulf War as a solution to Syria; however, there was a lot of thought that went into the 1st Gulf War and I do not see the same attention being put into Syrian Policy Making.

Therefore, I favor the need for more brains, than bombs and boots on the ground in Syria. I feel that it would serve humanity far more if we could reach out to the Muslim community and focus on the reality that radical Muslim's are becoming monsters as opposed to martyrs and are in essence contrary to God...

Those of you that have read this I hope that you appreciate my thoughts on Syria, my suggestions to "United Nations "Humanitarian Intervention" into Libya, my thoughts on how the Russian VETO in the United Nations Security Council in support of Assad/Syria came about.

I hope that Russia can become a more constructive partner and stop supporting Mass Murders as they have in Syria, Ukraine and even Libya.

Lastly, I hope that you appreciate my thoughts and great concerns for a "Grand Coalition Intervention in Syria to reduce Terrorism, because I do not think it is well thought out.

To repeat, I feel that the Syrian coalition concept is being compared to my planning and organizing the multinational coalition during the 1st Gulf War; however, there was a lot of thought that went into the 1st Gulf War and I do not see the same attention being put into Syrian Policy Making; in fact I favor the need for more brains than bombs and boots on the ground in Syria.

Therefore, I favor the need for more brains, than bombs and boots on the ground in Syria. I feel that it would serve humanity far more if we could reach out to the Muslim community and focus on the reality that radical Muslim's are becoming monsters as opposed to martyrs and are in essence contrary to God...

Only changing the mindsets of those that are easily influenced can we change the world for the better; be it in Syria or our poorest neighborhoods around the world those choose crime and corruption over education and creating constructive growth and development within their communities... People must develop themselves to develop their communities...

I hope you were informed by my Expert Opinion on Syria, Terrorism and United Nations Partner Policy Making...

In short I have followed the Syrian issue since the beginning. I feel that my United Nations "Humanitarian Intervention" into Libya had quite an impact on the "Failed Policies" that occurred in Syria after a Russian VETO in the United Nations Security Council. Russia grandstanded about how Gadhafi was brutally killed and how the U.N. overstepping authority of the resolution.

This compares and contrast Libya with Syria and we see that despite Libya turning into a failed state the "Humanitarian Intervention" did not follow my suggestions completely, nor did U.N. accept a "Divide Libya" Policy it still outweighs the support of al Assad's "Mass Murders" and a 5 year Civil War that has cost nearly 350,000 lives and about 4.5 million refugees fleeing Syria...

Negotiations continue "5 Years later" with Secretary of State Kerry leading the way...

SYRIA

THE UNITED NATIONS
ON VACATION

BY

HARVEY CARROLL, JR.
"THE UNELECTED PRESIDENT"

I'm a former U.S. Army Military Policeman/Investigator, whom became a "Political Junkie" for the past three ...

I now hold a Bachelors of Business Administration Degree specializing in Real Estate and Finance, and three partial Masters in Business, Public Administration as well as Diplomacy and International Commerce...

I've been considered the most influential international political figure in Kentucky-US, and some would say that perhaps in the World at one time. I have dealt with Governors, Senators, Presidents and Foreign Heads of State; and in the process I have saved millions of lives, and affected the economic fate of nations... Yet, I have made mistakes, and even cost lives and often ponder if the "End Justified the Means."

It has always been quite easy for me to deal with complex U.S. National and International Policy. From a young age I dealt with local, state, national and international policy that includes Latin America i.e. "Panama," Middle East (Iraq, Libya, Syria, Israel, Iran), Africa, and even coming to the AID after the collapse of the Soviet Union to protect U.S. and Global Security by suggesting buying out the nuclear weapons to prevent them from ending up on the Black Market for Terrorism, as well as preventing the former fifteen Soviet States against each other.

I also suggested financial bailouts, and another financial AID via the IFC/World Bank for Ukraine that saved seventy-five banks a few years ago (a similar plan presented to the U.S. House and Senate Financial Services Committee "Frank and Dodd" to bailout the American Economy to assist 2/3rds of the American States and Top Banks from Collapse.

More recently, I have shared suggestions to have the OSCE get between the separatist and the Ukrainian Army to the Ukrainian Presidents people tasked to negotiate the Minsk Agreements that may have prevented Ukraine from turning into another Syria... I've also offered up a "Crimean Compromise" that could solve the issues between Ukraine, Russia and the occupied territory of Crimea...

31254301R00088

Printed in Great Britain
by Amazon